string class

fingerboard geo[illegible]

an intonation, note-reading, theory, shifting system

by barbara barber

ISBN 0-7390-5025-7

Preludio Music Inc.
exclusively distributed by
Alfred Publishing Co., Inc.
PO Box 10003
Van Nuys, CA 91410-0003

Contents

Principles of Fingerboard Geography

1. Finger Patterns, or intervallic relationships, consist of various vertical combinations of whole-steps and half-steps on the fingerboard.

2. When two or more fingers are placed on the fingerboard, a Finger Pattern must be established.

3. If fewer than four fingers are used, the missing finger/s may be filled in to determine the Finger Pattern.

4. **In all exercises in this book, use block fingering, anchoring all fingers wherever possible.** This allows the player to *hear, see,* and *feel* the Finger Patterns.

5. The color assigned to each Finger Pattern reflects the tonality of the pattern.

6. A Finger Pattern may be played on any one string or combination of two, three, or four strings, producing double-stops and chords.

7. Every double-stop and chord is a Finger Pattern. Remember to fill in any missing fingers to establish questionable patterns.

8. When playing double-stops and chords, the differential, or horizontal distance between the fingers, feels slightly larger, especially in half-steps.

9. A Finger Pattern may be played in any position on the fingerboard.

10. Finger Patterns become proportionately smaller as they move up the fingerboard and larger as they move down. In shifting, the hand frame constantly expands and contracts. Remember to fill in any missing fingers to establish questionable patterns.

11. Finger Patterns are the same on any size violin viola, cello or bass; only the proportions change.

12. For easy reference, the Finger Pattern charts may be posted in the teacher's studio, the classroom or the student's practice area. We recommend laminating or inserting the charts into plastic sheet protectors for long-term use.

13. Playing the violin, viola, cello or bass in tune is never easy. Hearing, seeing and feeling Finger Patterns can take the guesswork out of intonation and eliminate the need for fingerboard tapes.

14. Finger Patterns are used for life!

For more advanced Finger Pattern and Fingerboard Geography studies, see

Violin Fingerboard Geography, Volumes 1 and 2

and

Viola Fingerboard Geography, Volumes 1 and 2

by Barbara Barber

Published by Preludio Music Inc.

Distributed by Alfred Publishing Co., Inc.

Part 1: Finger Marches

The 1st finger is the "home base" note on which all Finger Patterns are built. The 1st Finger Marches in this section establish the string player's left hand placement in 1st position with the "high" 1st finger and teach the hand to move across the fingerboard from high strings to low and back again (the opposite for bass). 1st Finger Marches are excellent for beginning string students or those who have just moved to a larger size instrument. Finger Marches may be played between any open string and 2nd, 3rd or 4th fingers, between any 2 fingers, and in any position. They can also be played on 1, 2 or 3 strings only. At a later time, 1st Finger Marches using the "low" 1st finger may be introduced. Mixed 1st Marches alternate between the high and low 1st fingers, zigzagging diagonally across the strings. Zigzagging Finger Marches are especially useful when students encounter *changing* Finger Patterns such as in Nos. 4 though 8 below in which a finger moves diagonally across the fingerboard. Teachers and students can invent Finger Marches as needed in the repertoire. Here are a few examples:

Additional Exercises

High 1st Finger Marches

Violin

Viola

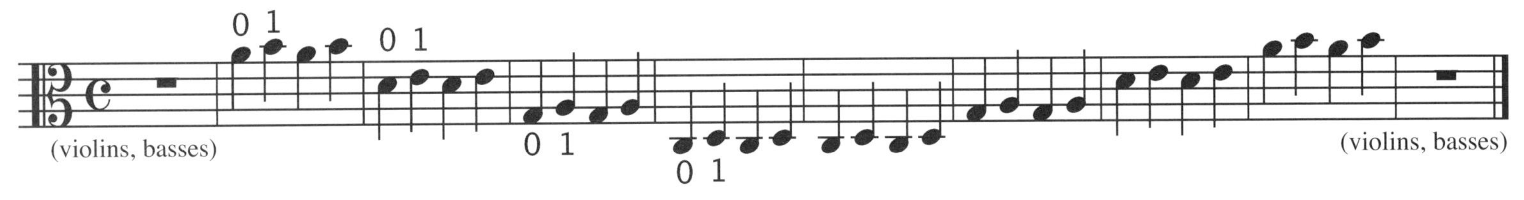

Cello

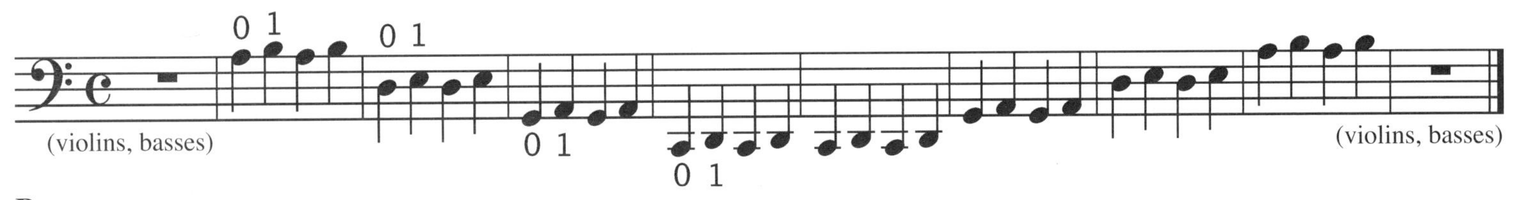

Bass

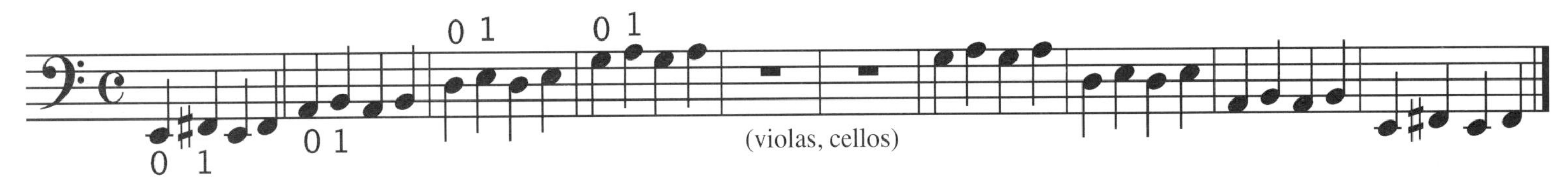

Low 1st Finger Marches

Violin

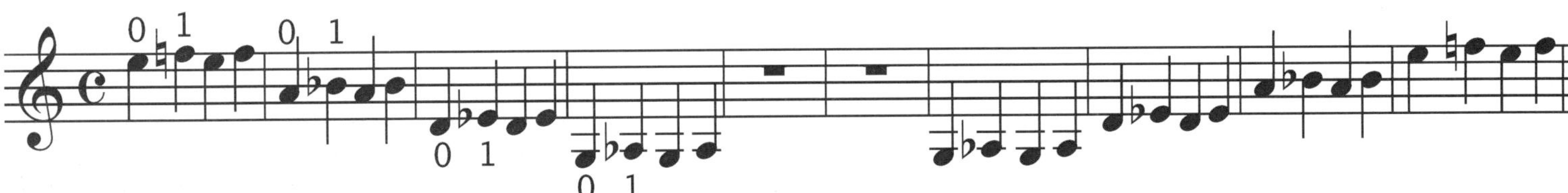

Viola

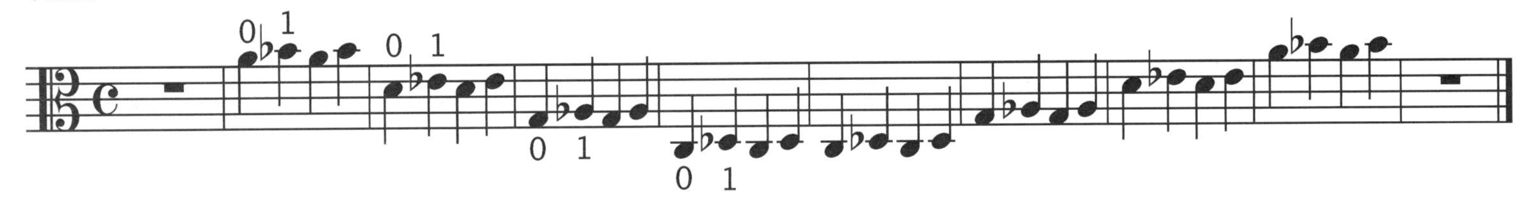

Cello

Bass

Mixed 1st Finger Marches

♩ = 88

Watch the 1st Finger as it zigzags diagonally across the strings!

Violin

Viola

Cello

Bass

Part 2: Four Basic Finger Patterns

To develop quick, precise action in the left hand, these short, "mini-scale" exercises in Part 2 should be played in the middle of the bow – the 8th notes with clean, staccato strokes and the 16th notes with detaché. The tempo is ♩ = 60. When used in the string class, start with the D string which will not require cellos and basses to shift. Each colored coded group of patterns is introduced from the highest string to the lowest (on bass, lowest to highest). When all four strings in any one color have been learned, violins and basses may play the E string exercise, violas and cellos join in for the A and D strings, and violas and cellos may play the C string exercise. Between each string, the teacher may prepare the next string or pattern by saying:

Introduction of the Green Pattern, usually the most difficult, especially on the lower strings, can be delayed until the students have mastered Red, Blue and Yellow.

Important: When playing Finger Pattern Exercises, violin and viola students should *always* use block fingering, leaving all fingers anchored. Violas may need to lift 1st and 2nd fingers for the Green Pattern only. Cello and bass students should keep fingers anchored *wherever possible.* While block fingering is not always used when playing repertoire, keeping fingers anchored in this intonation system allows the student to *see, hear* and *feel* the patterns.

There are many variations that may be used with these Finger Pattern Exercises. Each exercise can be repeated as many times as needed. Students especially enjoy playing them in canon. The 2nd group starts at measure 2:

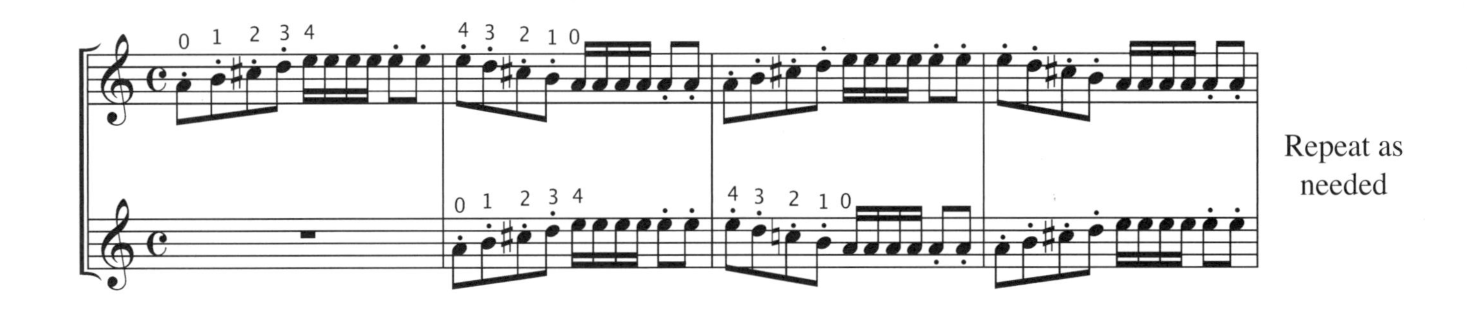

When students become familiar with two or more patterns, they can change the pattern at the top of the ascending scale, then play a different pattern in the descending scale.

Go up the scale in Red, stop, lift 2nd finger C♯, move it to C♮, come down the scale in Blue:

Play this first with a stop, then without.

Finger Patterns may be played one ½ step lower, with the first finger on E♭ in 1st position. The Yellow and Green Patterns frequently start on the "low" 1st finger in 1st position.

Yellow Finger Pattern with 1st finger on E♭:

Green Finger Pattern with 1st finger on E♭:

As an introduction to string crossings, double-stops and chords, distribute the fingers on two, three, and four strings.

Violins should keep all fingers anchored!

Blue pattern on two strings:

Blue pattern on three strings:

Blue pattern on four strings:

Violins should keep all fingers anchored!

By changing the Finger Patterns in the ascending/descending scales and distributing the fingers on 1, 2, 3, and 4 strings, a variety of combinations are possible. Be creative!

Violin Red Pattern

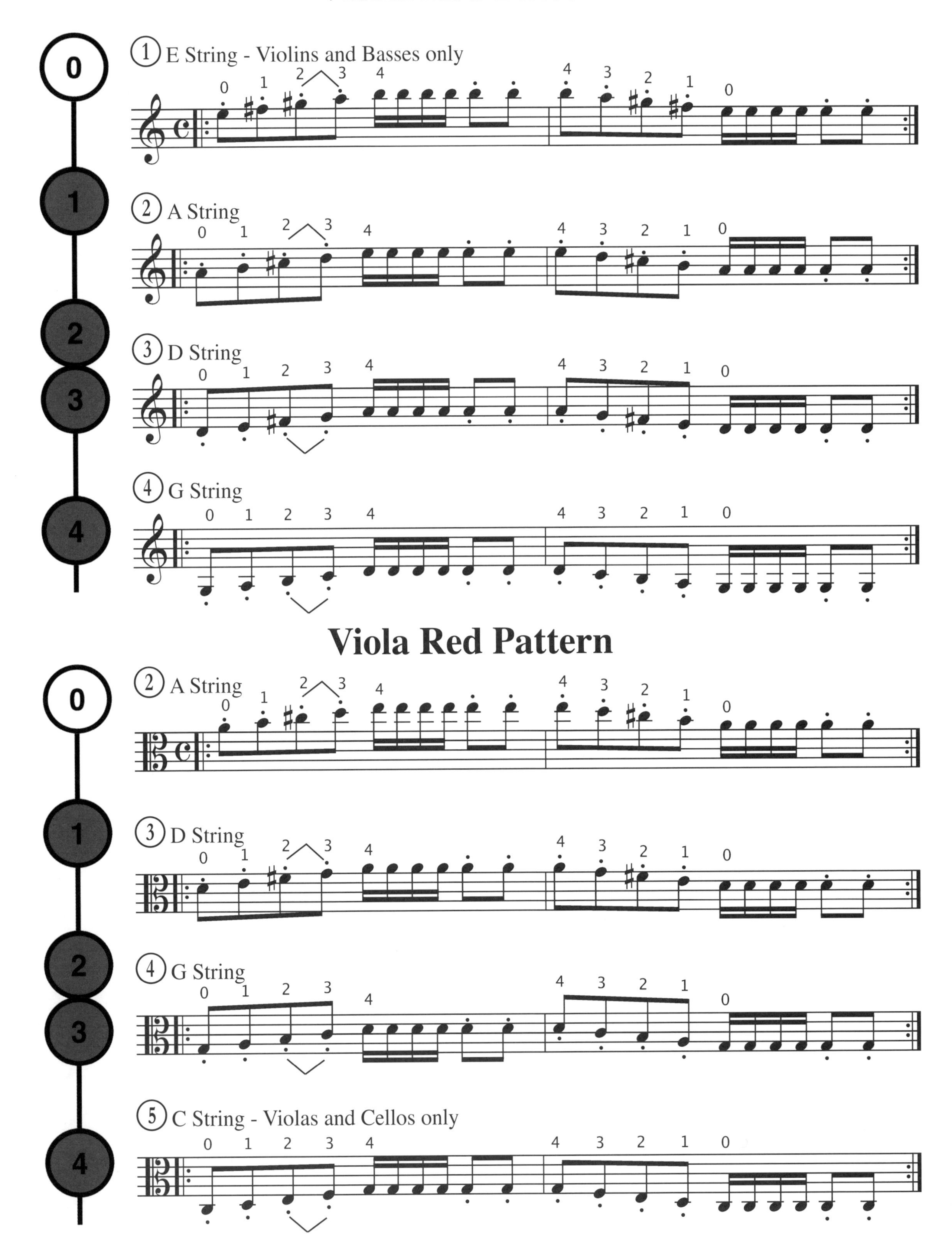

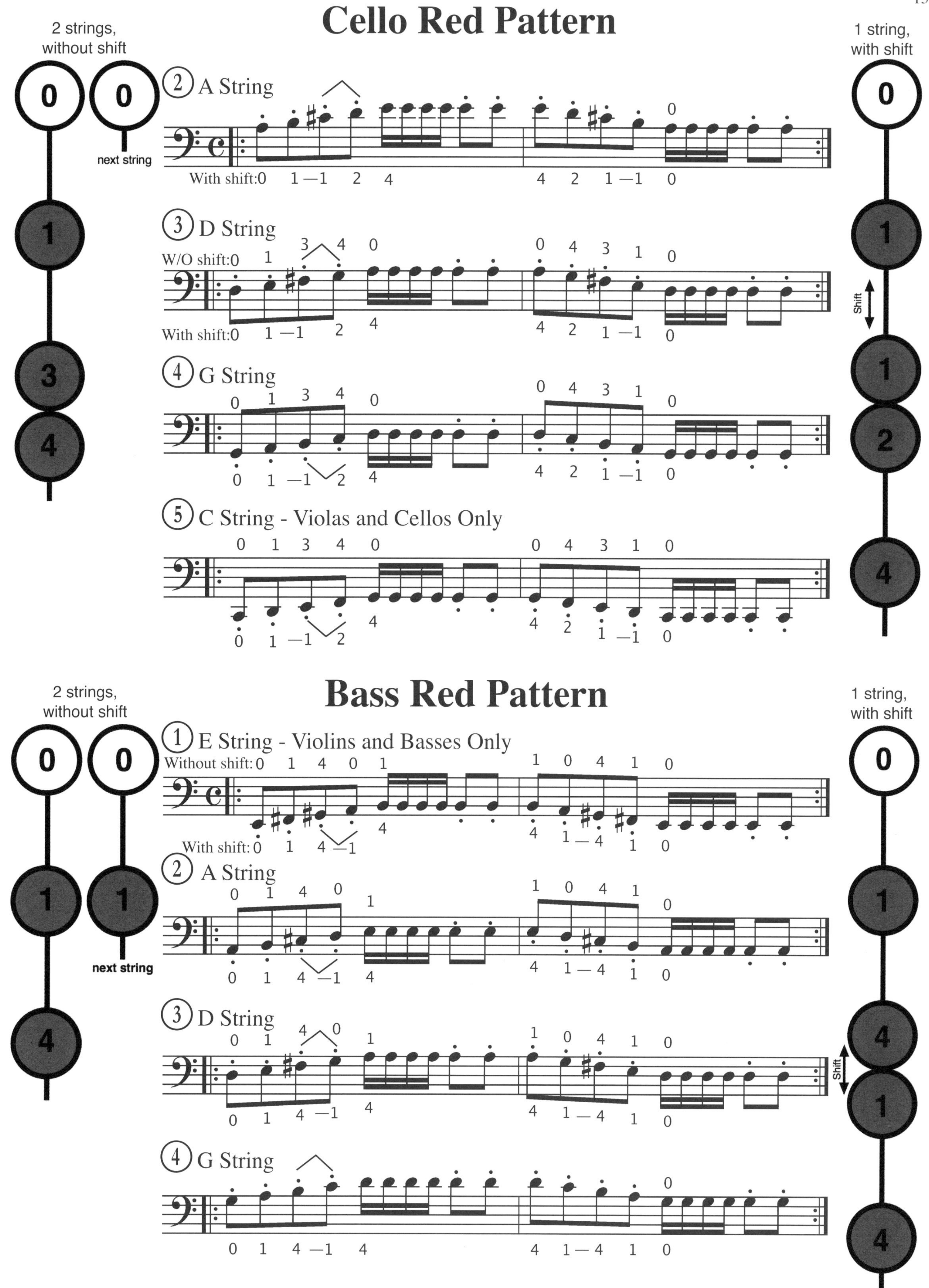
Cello Red Pattern
2 strings, without shift
next string
1 string, with shift
Shift
② A String
With shift: 0 1 —1 2 4
4 2 1 —1 0
③ D String
W/O shift: 0 1 3 4 0
0 4 3 1 0
With shift: 0 1 —1 2 4
4 2 1 —1 0
④ G String
0 1 3 4 0
0 4 3 1 0
0 1 —1 2 4
4 2 1 —1 0
⑤ C String - Violas and Cellos Only
0 1 3 4 0
0 4 3 1 0
0 1 —1 2 4
4 2 1 —1 0
Bass Red Pattern
2 strings, without shift
next string
1 string, with shift
Shift
① E String - Violins and Basses Only
Without shift: 0 1 4 0 1
1 0 4 1 0
With shift: 0 1 4 —1 4
4 1 — 4 1 0
② A String
0 1 4 0 1
1 0 4 1 0
0 1 4 —1 4
4 1 — 4 1 0
③ D String
0 1 4 0 1
1 0 4 1 0
0 1 4 —1 4
4 1 — 4 1 0
④ G String
0
0 1 4 —1 4
4 1 — 4 1 0

Violin Blue Pattern

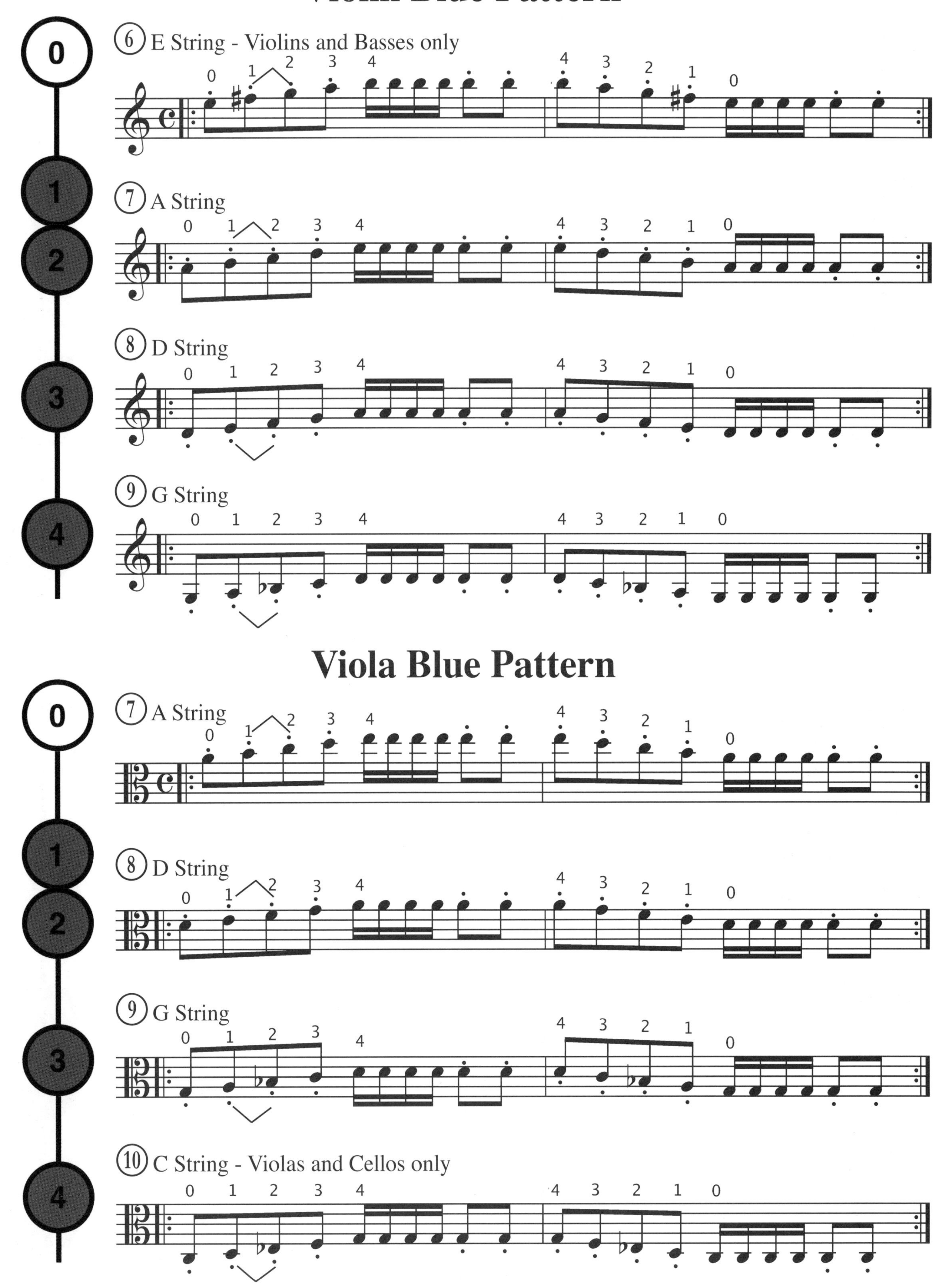

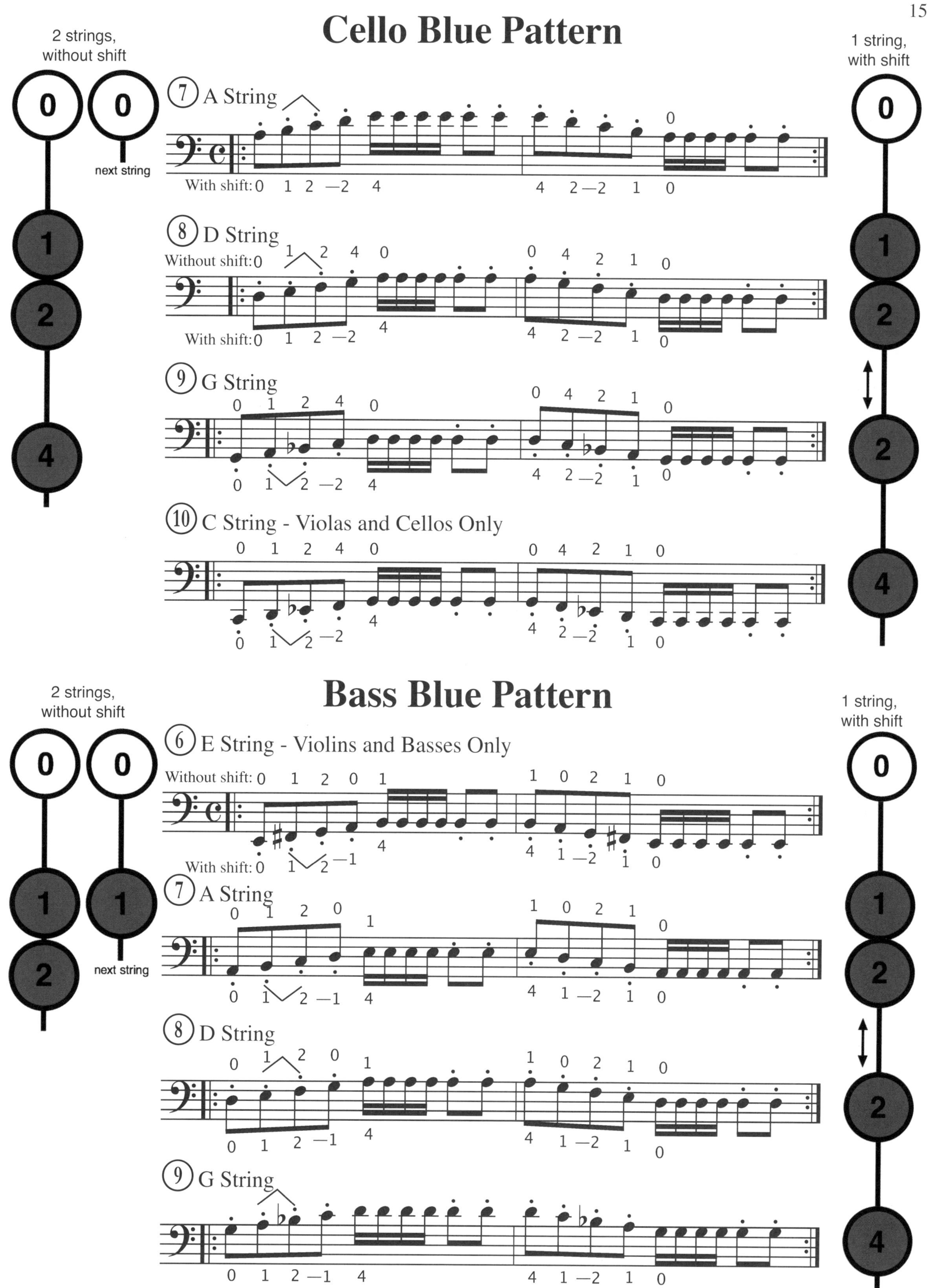
Cello Blue Pattern
2 strings, without shift
1 string, with shift
next string
7 A String
With shift: 0 1 2 —2 4 4 2—2 1 0
8 D String
Without shift: 0 1 2 4 0 0 4 2 1 0
With shift: 0 1 2 —2 4 4 2 —2 1 0
9 G String
10 C String - Violas and Cellos Only
Bass Blue Pattern
2 strings, without shift
1 string, with shift
next string
6 E String - Violins and Basses Only
Without shift: 0 1 2 0 1 1 0 2 1 0
With shift: 0 1 2 —1 4 4 1 —2 1 0
7 A String
8 D String
9 G String

Violin Yellow Pattern
11 E String - Violins and Basses only
0 1 2 3 4 4 3 2 1 0
12 A String
0 1 2 3 4 4 3 2 1 0
13 D String
0 1 2 3 4 4 3 2 1 0
14 G String
0 1 2 3 4 4 3 2 1 0
The 3rd finger in this pattern is "hot pink." It sounds, looks and feels very different!
Viola Yellow Pattern
12 A String
0 1 2 3 4 4 3 2 1 0
13 D String
0 1 2 3 4 4 3 2 1 0
14 G String
0 1 2 3 4 4 3 2 1 0
15 C String - Violas and Cellos only
0 1 2 3 4 4 3 2 1 0
0
1
2
3
4

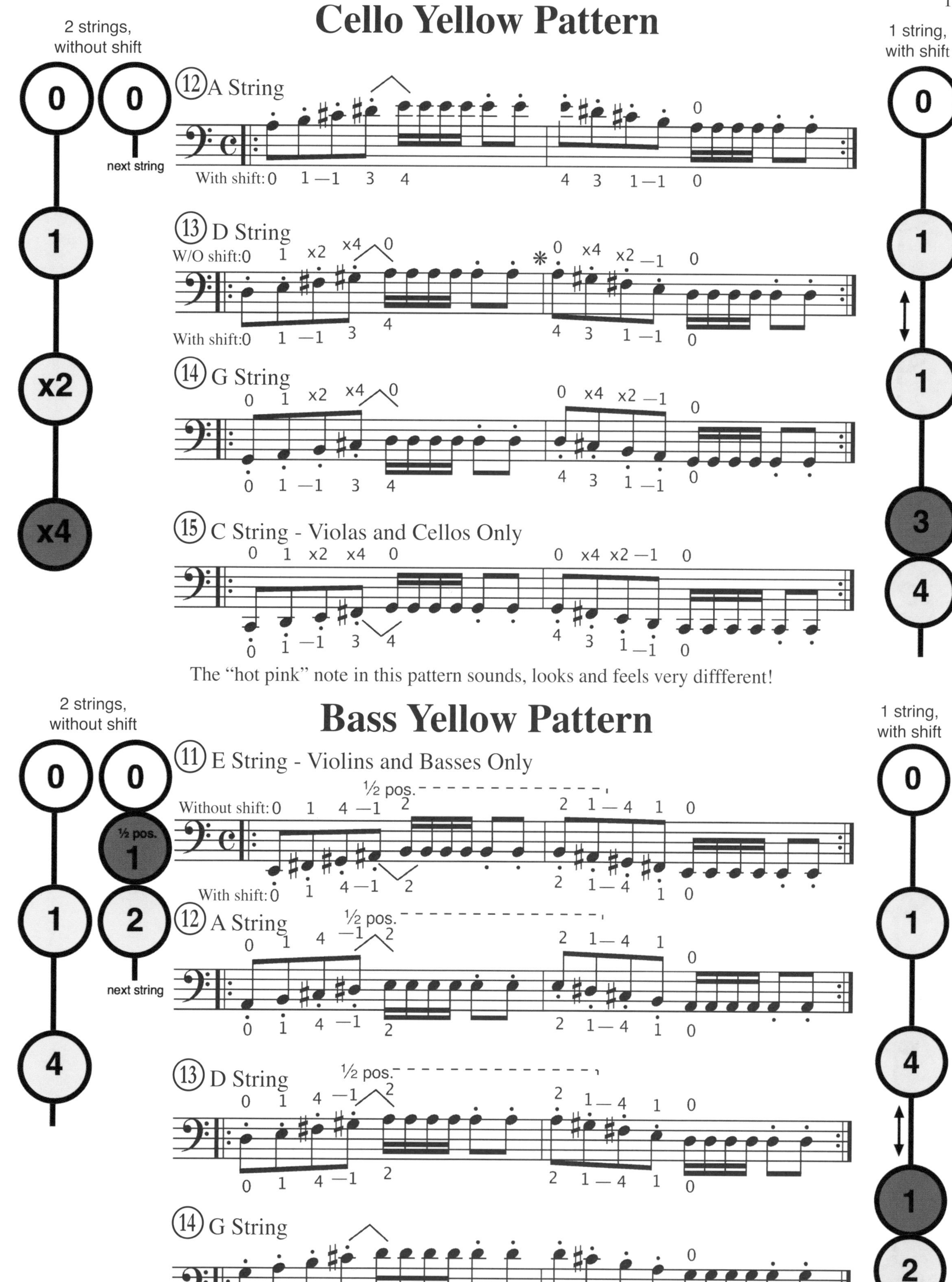
Cello Yellow Pattern
2 strings, without shift
next string
1 string, with shift
12 A String
With shift: 0 1 —1 3 4 4 3 1 —1 0
13 D String
W/O shift: 0 1 x2 x4 0 0 x4 x2 —1 0
With shift: 0 1 —1 3 4 4 3 1 —1 0
14 G String
15 C String - Violas and Cellos Only
The "hot pink" note in this pattern sounds, looks and feels very diffferent!
Bass Yellow Pattern
2 strings, without shift
½ pos.
next string
1 string, with shift
11 E String - Violins and Basses Only
½ pos.
Without shift: 0 1 4 —1 2 2 1 — 4 1 0
With shift: 0 1 4 —1 2 2 1 — 4 1 0
12 A String
½ pos.
13 D String
½ pos.
14 G String

Violin Green Pattern

0
1
2
3
4
16 E String - Violins and Basses only
0 1 2 3 4
4 3 2 1 0
17 A String
0 1 2 3 4
4 3 2 1 0
18 D String
0 1 2 3 4
4 3 2 1 0
19 G String
0 1 2 3 4
4 3 2 1 0
Viola Green Pattern
0
1
2
3
4
17 A String
0 1 2 3 4
4 3 2 1 0
18 D String
0 1 2 3 4
4 3 2 1 0
19 G String
0 1 2 3 4
4 3 2 1 0
20 C String - Violas and Cellos only
0 1 2 3 4
4 3 2 1 0

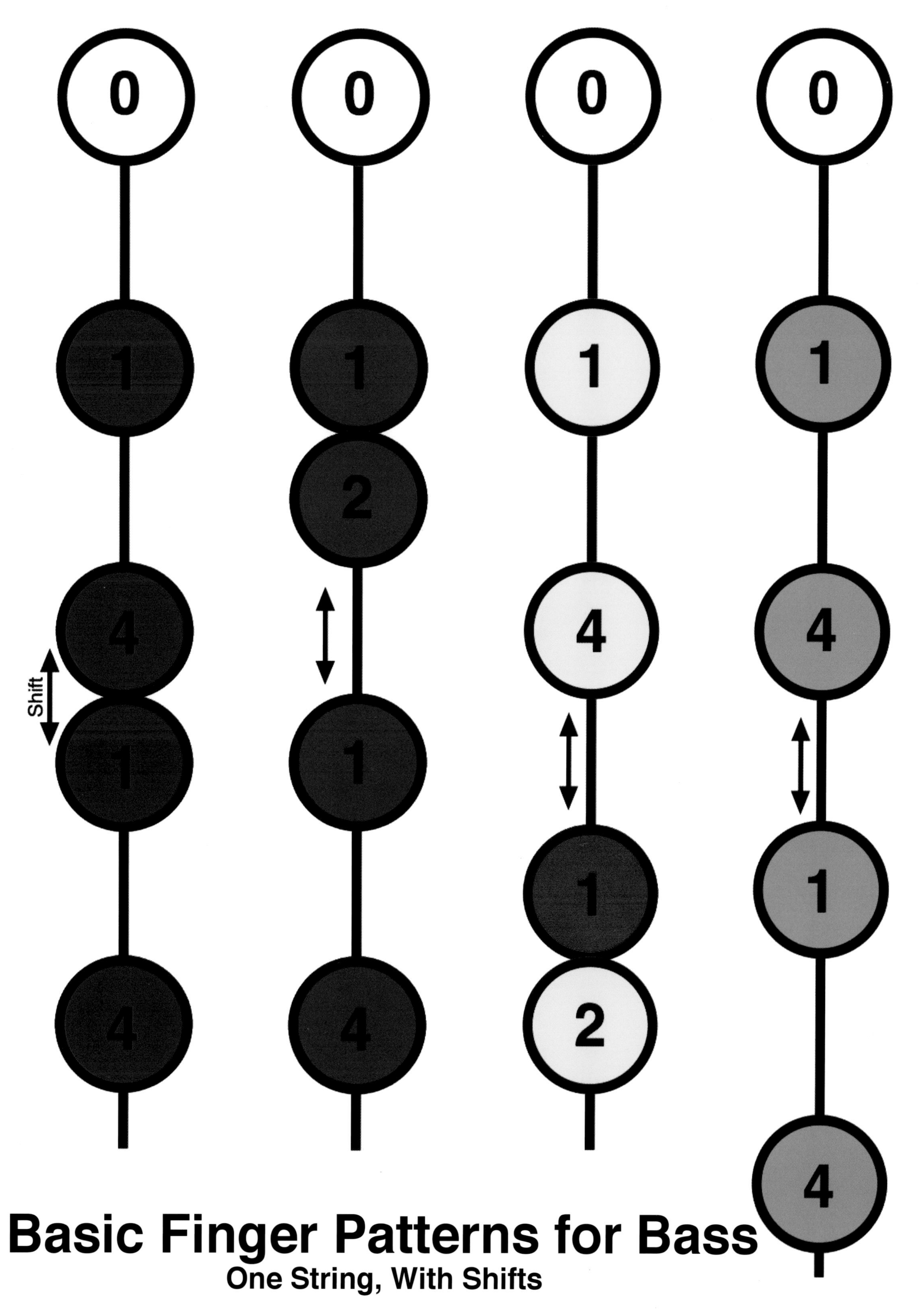

Basic Finger Patterns for Bass

One String, With Shifts

Basic Finger Patterns for Cello

Two Strings, Without Shifts

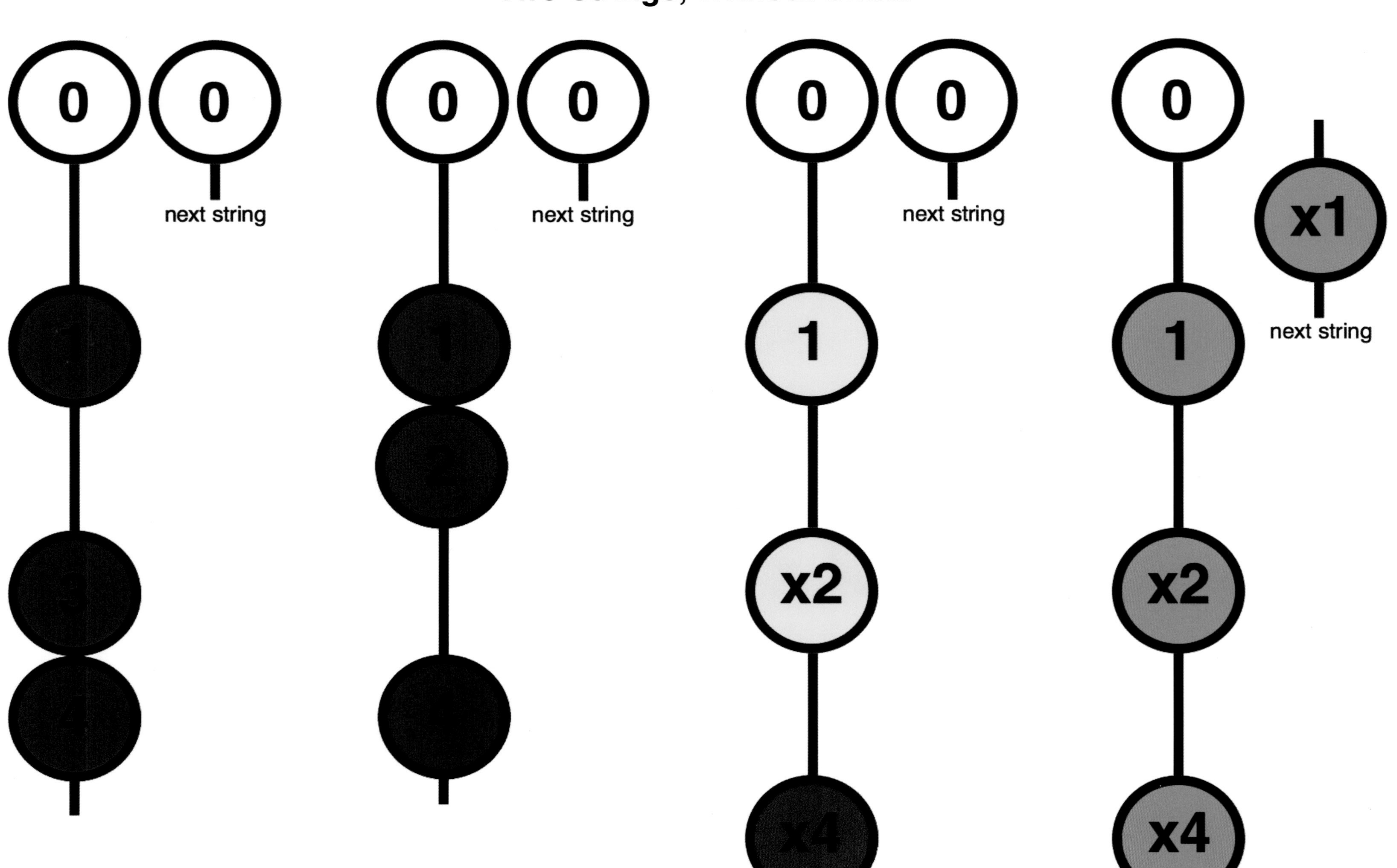

Basic Finger Patterns

Violin and Viola

Cello
Two Strings, Without Shifts

Cello
One String, With Shifts

Bass
Two Strings, Without Shifts

Bass
One String, With Shifts

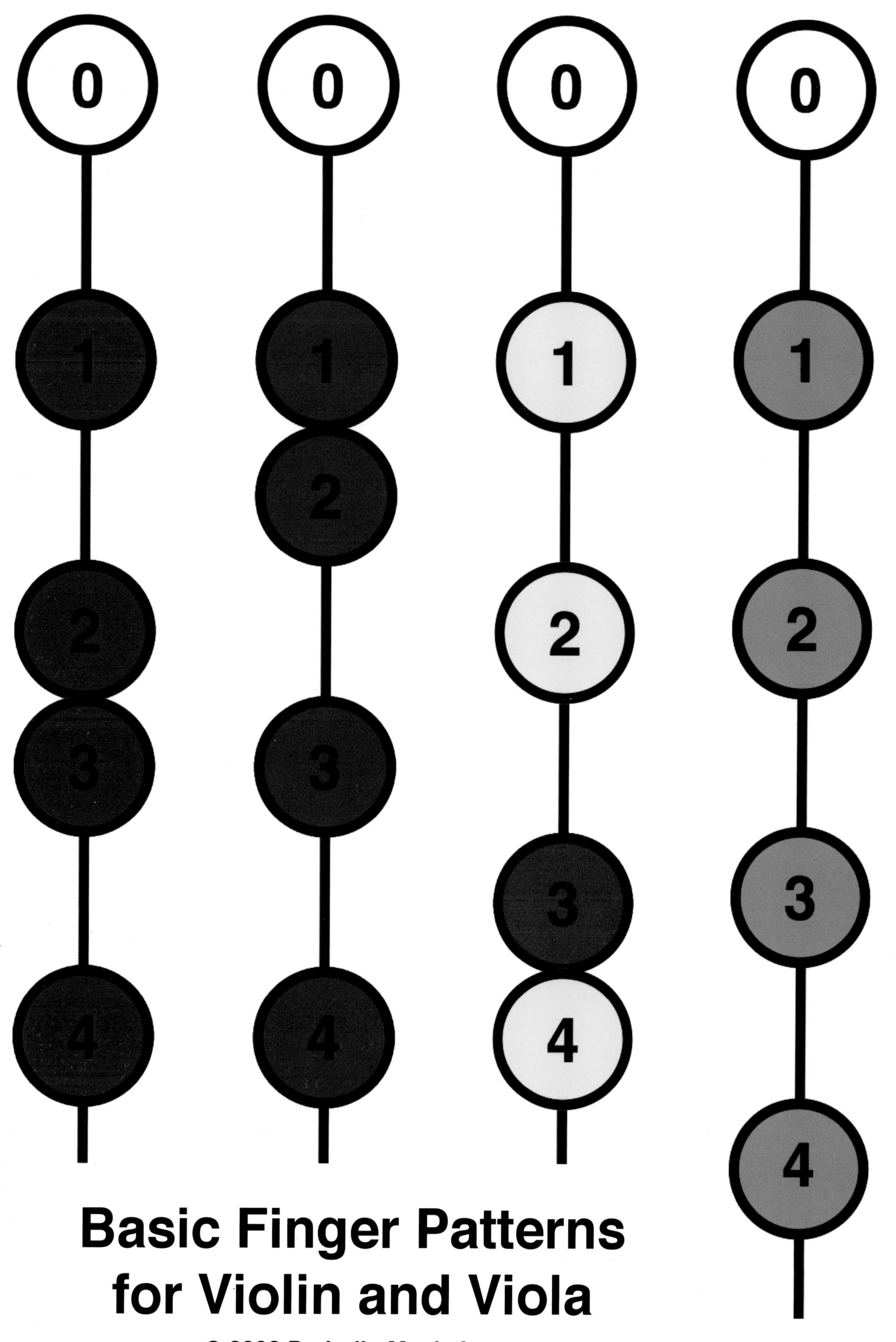

Basic Finger Patterns for Violin and Viola

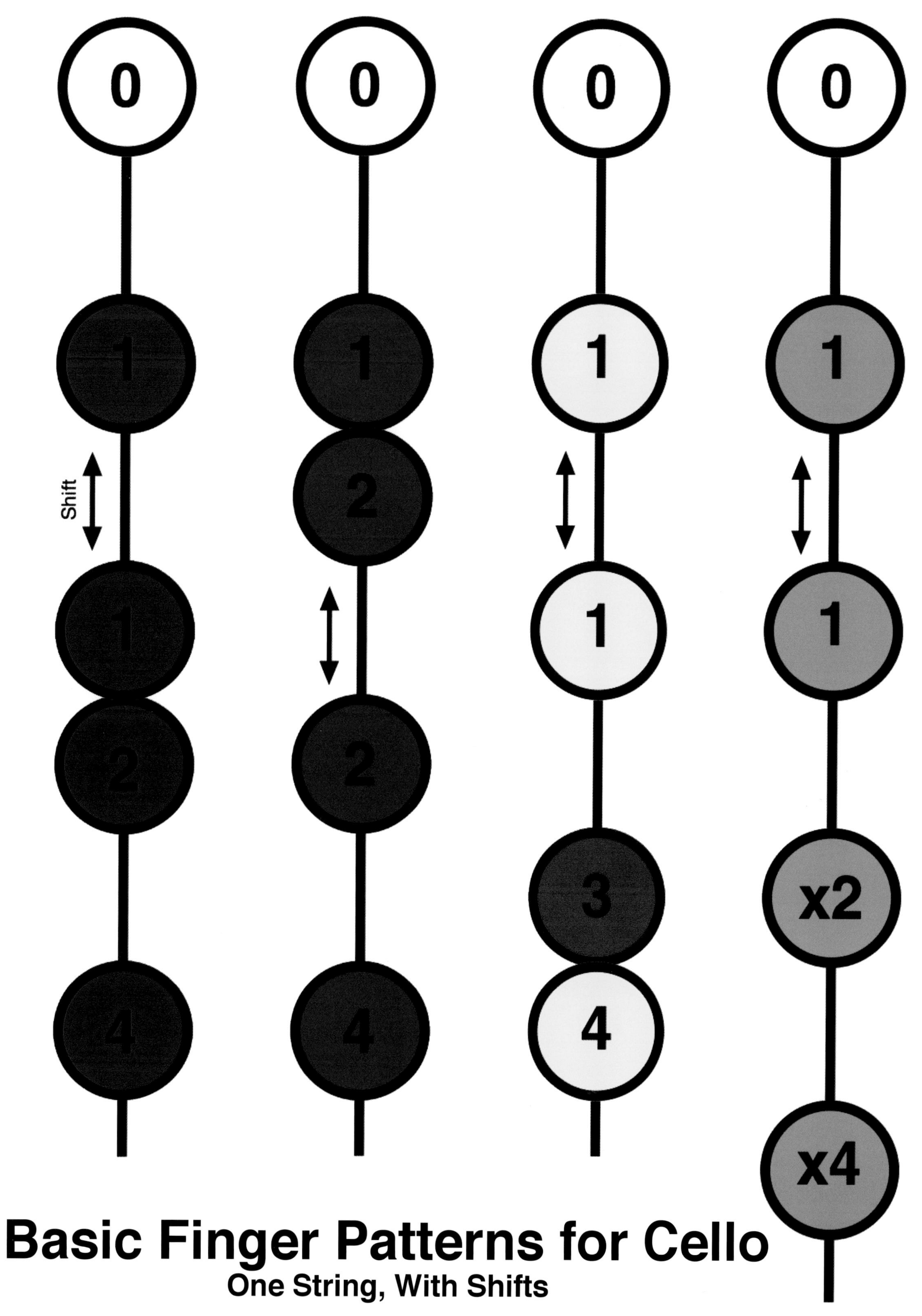

Basic Finger Patterns for Cello

One String, With Shifts

Basic Finger Patterns for Bass

Two Strings, Without Shifts

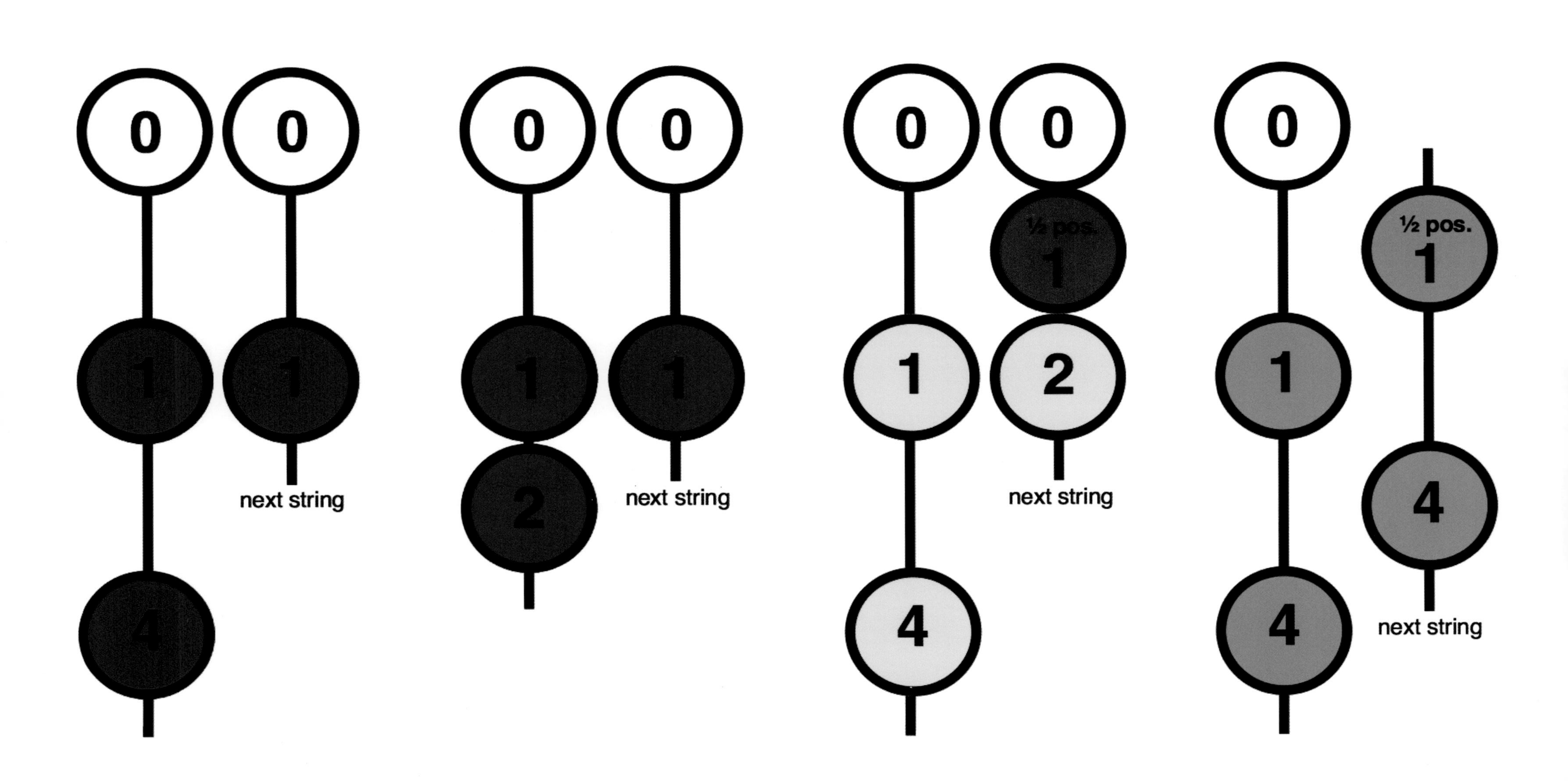

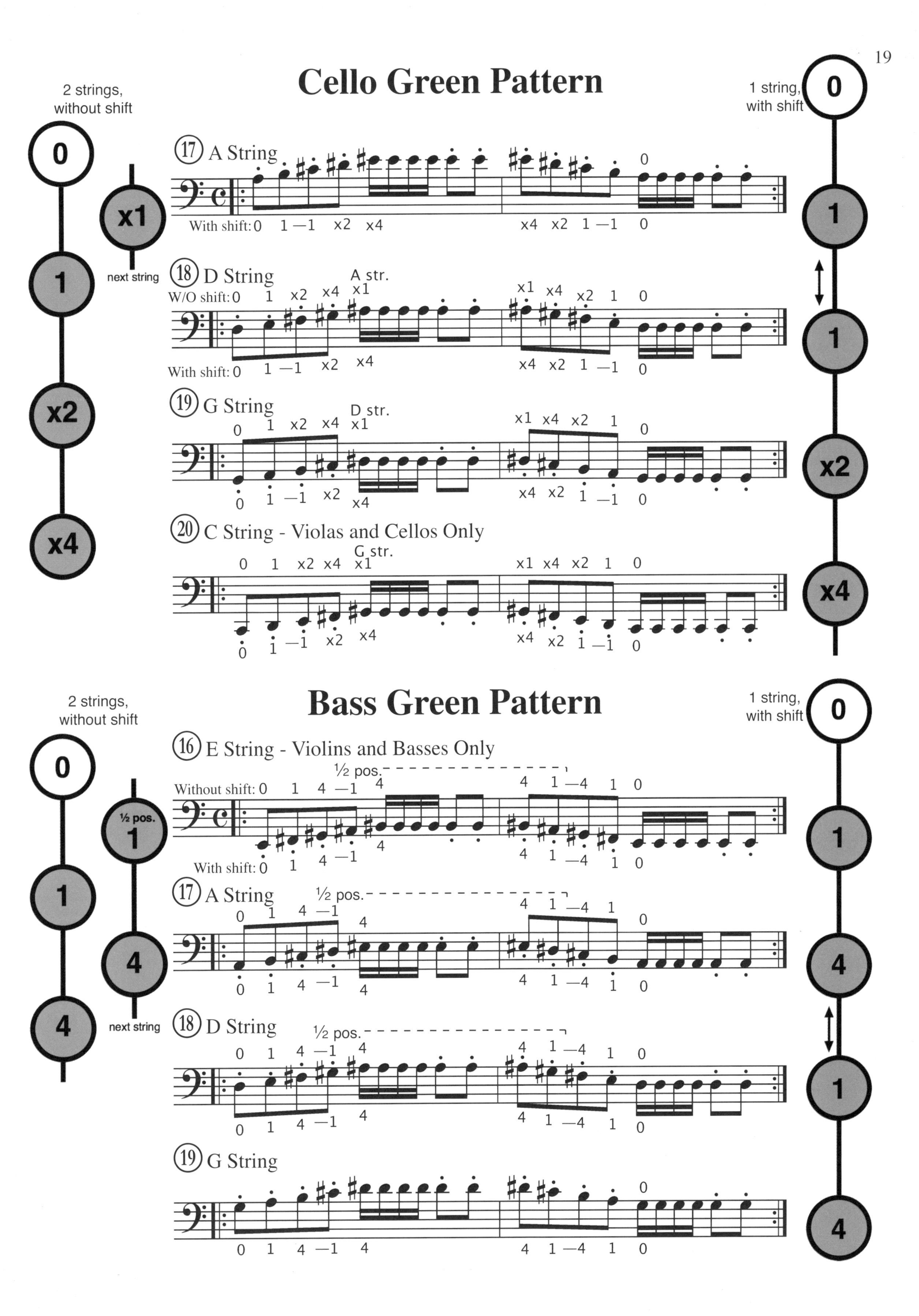
19
Cello Green Pattern
2 strings, without shift
1 string, with shift
0
x1
1
next string
x2
x4
17 A String
With shift: 0 1 —1 x2 x4
x4 x2 1 —1 0
18 D String
A str.
W/O shift: 0 1 x2 x4 x1
x1 x4 x2 1 0
With shift: 0 1 —1 x2 x4
x4 x2 1 —1 0
19 G String
D str.
0 1 x2 x4 x1
x1 x4 x2 1 0
0 1 —1 x2 x4
x4 x2 1 —1 0
20 C String - Violas and Cellos Only
G str.
0 1 x2 x4 x1
x1 x4 x2 1 0
0 1 —1 x2 x4
x4 x2 1 —1 0
Bass Green Pattern
2 strings, without shift
1 string, with shift
0
½ pos. 1
1
4
next string
16 E String - Violins and Basses Only
½ pos.
Without shift: 0 1 4 —1 4
4 1 —4 1 0
With shift: 0 1 4 —1 4
4 1 —4 1 0
17 A String
½ pos.
0 1 4 —1 4
4 1 —4 1 0
0 1 4 —1 4
4 1 —4 1 0
18 D String
½ pos.
0 1 4 —1 4
4 1 —4 1 0
0 1 4 —1 4
4 1 —4 1 0
19 G String
0
0 1 4 —1 4
4 1 —4 1 0

Part 3: Fingerboard Geography

This section introduces all of the notes in 1st position for violins and violas. In the string class, start on the D string to avoid shifting for violins and violas. Cellos and basses, however, are required to shift in Part 3. The tempo is ♩ = 60 and the exercises should be played with full, legato bow strokes. Students should "see and say" the note names before playing each pair of notes in the left column. Next the students "see and say" the distance on the fingerboard in the center column, then play. Finally the students "see and say" the name of the interval in the right column, then play. These three steps can be introduced over a period of days, weeks, or months, depending on the level of the students and the frequency of lessons/classes. When the students have learned the information in all three columns, go to the same exercises on pages 26-29, naming notes, distances and intervals by reading the notes only. For variety, go around a circle or down a row of students, asking each to name either note names, distance on the fingerboard or name of the interval, then everyone plays the pair of notes. Later, the first student says the note names, the second student says the distance on the fingerboard, the third student says the name of the interval, then all play the pair of notes. In a class of mixed levels, less advanced students can say note names and more advanced ones say distance and interval.

When playing Fingerboard Geography, care must be taken to ensure smooth and efficient finger actions such as anchoring and sliding chromatically. Violins and violas should keep the 1st finger anchored on the lower string for the first line and on both strings for the second line. The Major 3rd and tri-tone intervals in the first line can be filled in with the missing fingers as shown, to establish these patterns. The 2nd and 3rd fingers will stay anchored as they are placed in the second line. The 2nd and 3rd fingers should slide on the upper string in chromatic motions such as C to C♯, then remain anchored. When playing C♯ to D, the 2nd finger should "touch and lift" – the 3rd is placed, then 2nd is lifted; likewise with D♯ to E.

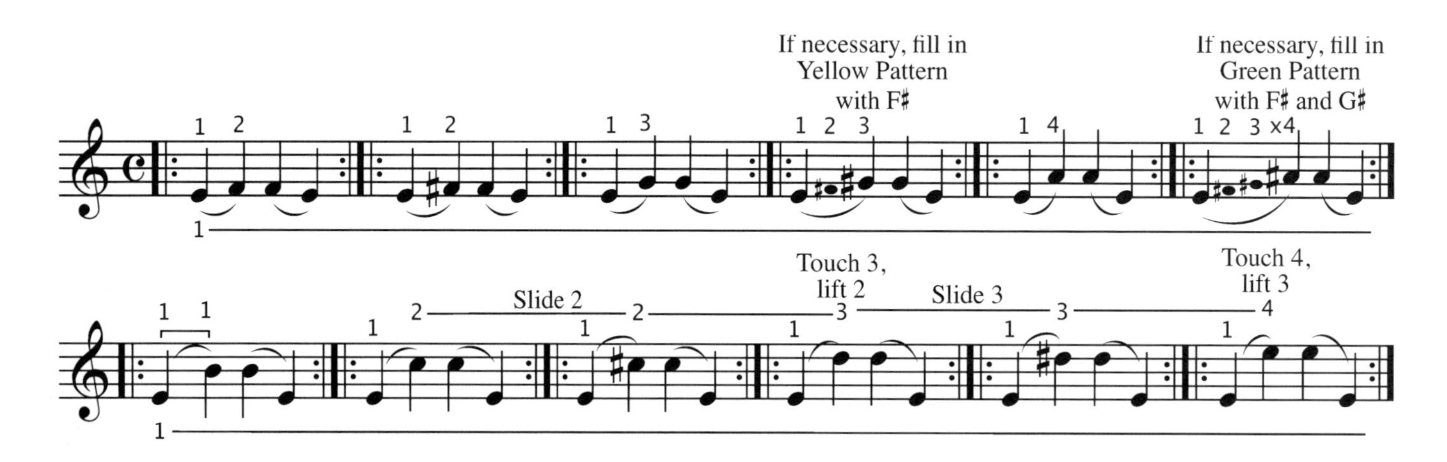

Additional Exercises

Violin Notes on D & A Strings in 1st Position

Note Names & Location on the Staff	Distance on the Fingerboard	Name of the Interval
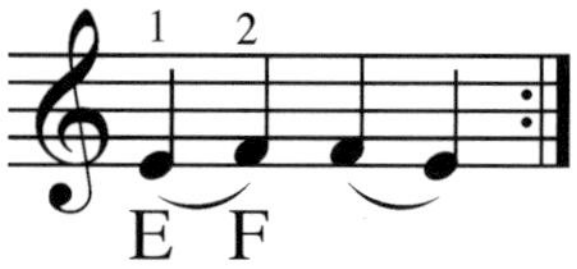 1 2 E F	½ step	minor 2nd
 1 2 E F♯	whole-step	Major 2nd
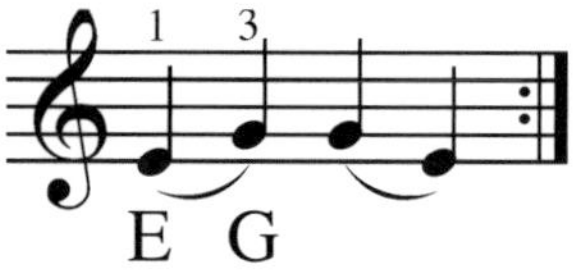 1 3 E G	1½ steps	minor 3rd
 1 3 E G♯	2 whole-steps	Major 3rd
 1 4 E A	2½ steps	Perfect 4th
 1 x4 E A♯	3 whole-steps	Tri-tone (Augmented 4th to A♯, Diminished 5th to B♭)
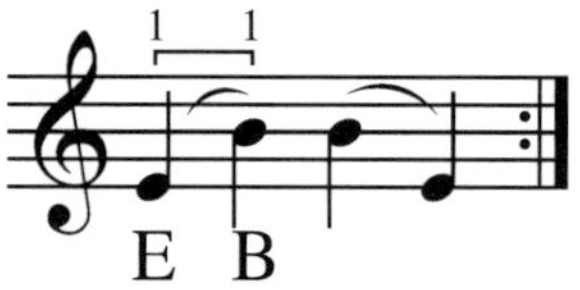 1 1 E B	straight across	Perfect 5th
 1 2 E C	½ step	minor 6th
 1 2 E C♯	whole-step	Major 6th
 1 3 E D	1½ steps	minor 7th
 1 3 E D♯	2 whole-steps	Major 7th
 1 4 E E	2½ steps	Perfect 8va (octave)

Viola Notes on D & A Strings in 1st Position

Note Names & Location on the Staff	Distance on the Fingerboard	Name of the Interval
 1 2 E F	½ step	minor 2nd
 1 2 E F♯	whole-step	Major 2nd
 1 3 E G	1½ steps	minor 3rd
 1 3 E G♯	2 whole-steps	Major 3rd
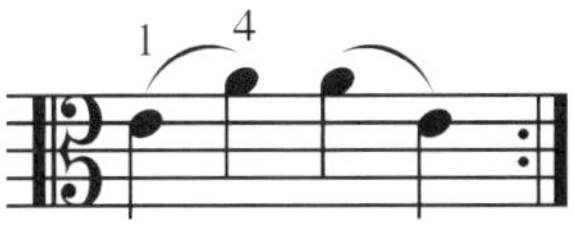 1 4 E A	2½ steps	Perfect 4th
 1 x4 E A♯	3 whole-steps	Tri-tone (Augmented 4th to A♯, Diminished 5th to B♭)
 1 1 E B	straight across	Perfect 5th
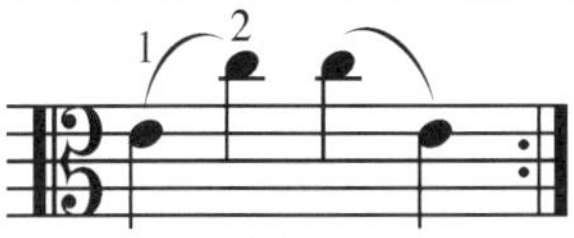 1 2 E C	½ step	minor 6th
 1 2 E C♯	whole-step	Major 6th
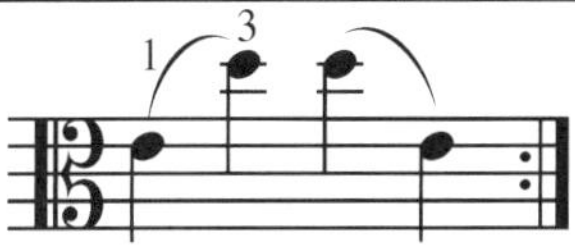 1 3 E D	1½ steps	minor 7th
 1 3 E D♯	2 whole-steps	Major 7th
 1 4 E E	2½ steps	Perfect 8va (octave)

Cello Notes on D & A Strings Starting in 1st Position

Note Names & Location on the Staff	Distance on the Fingerboard	Name of the Interval
 E F	½ step	minor 2nd
 E F♯	whole-step	Major 2nd
 E G	1½ steps	minor 3rd
 E G♯	2 whole-steps	Major 3rd
 E A	2½ steps	Perfect 4th
 E A♯	3 whole-steps	Tri-tone (Augmented 4th to A♯, Diminished 5th to B♭)
 E B	straight across	Perfect 5th
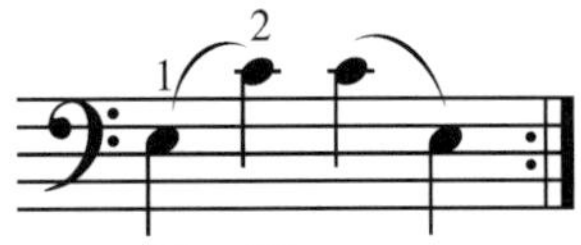 E C	½ step	minor 6th
 E C♯	whole-step	Major 6th
 E D	1½ steps	minor 7th
 E D♯	2 whole-steps	Major 7th
 E E	2½ steps	Perfect 8va (octave)

Bass Notes on D & G Strings Starting in 1st Position

Note Names & Location on the Staff	Distance on the Fingerboard	Name of the Interval
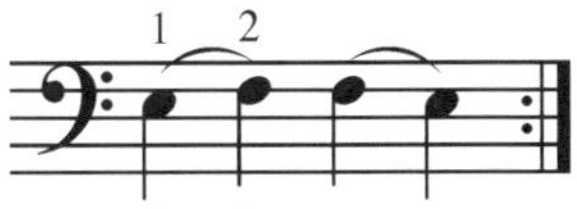 1 2 E F	1/2 step	minor 2nd
 1 4 E F♯	whole-step	Major 2nd
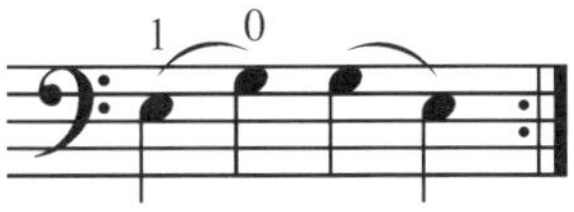 1 0 E G	1 1/2 steps	minor 3rd
 1 1 E G♯	2 whole-steps	Major 3rd
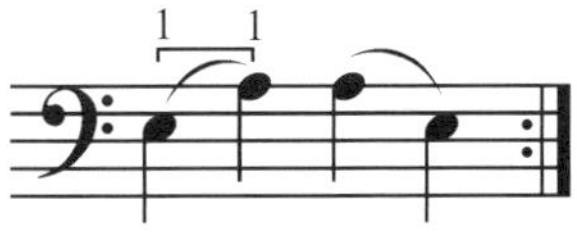 1 1 E A	straight across	Perfect 4th
 1 2 E A♯	1/2 step	Tri-tone (Augmented 4th to A♯, Diminished 5th to B♭)
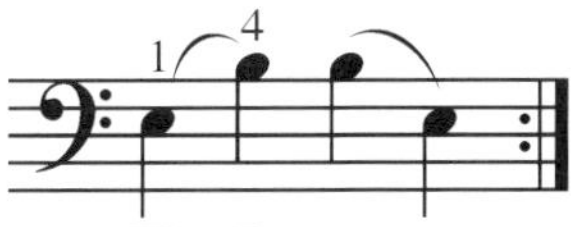 1 4 E B	whole step	Perfect 5th
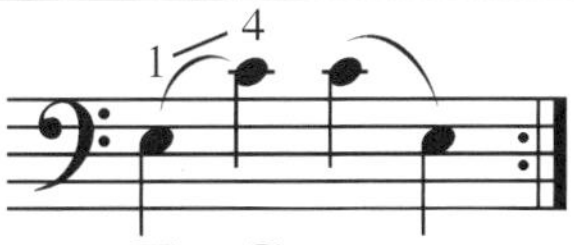 1 4 E C	1 1/2 steps	minor 6th
 1 4 E C♯	2 whole-steps	Major 6th
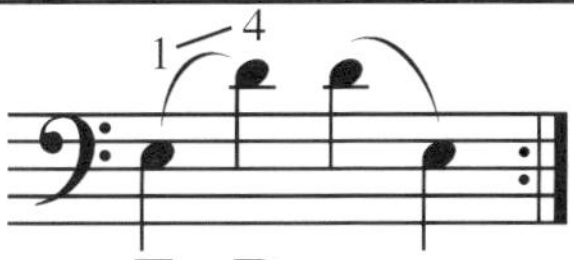 1 4 E D	2 1/2 steps	minor 7th
 1 4 E D♯	3 whole-steps	Major 7th
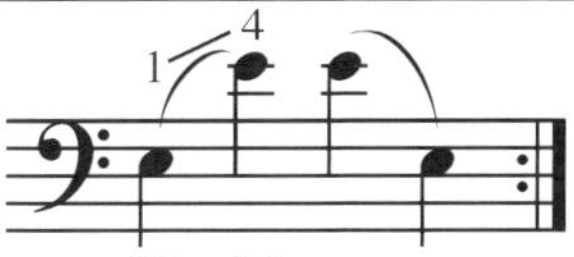 1 4 E E	3 1/2 steps	Perfect 8va (octave)

Violin Fingerboard Geography

Viola Fingerboard Geography

♩ = 60

① **Violins and Basses on E string starting on F♯**

② **A String starting on B - shifting required**

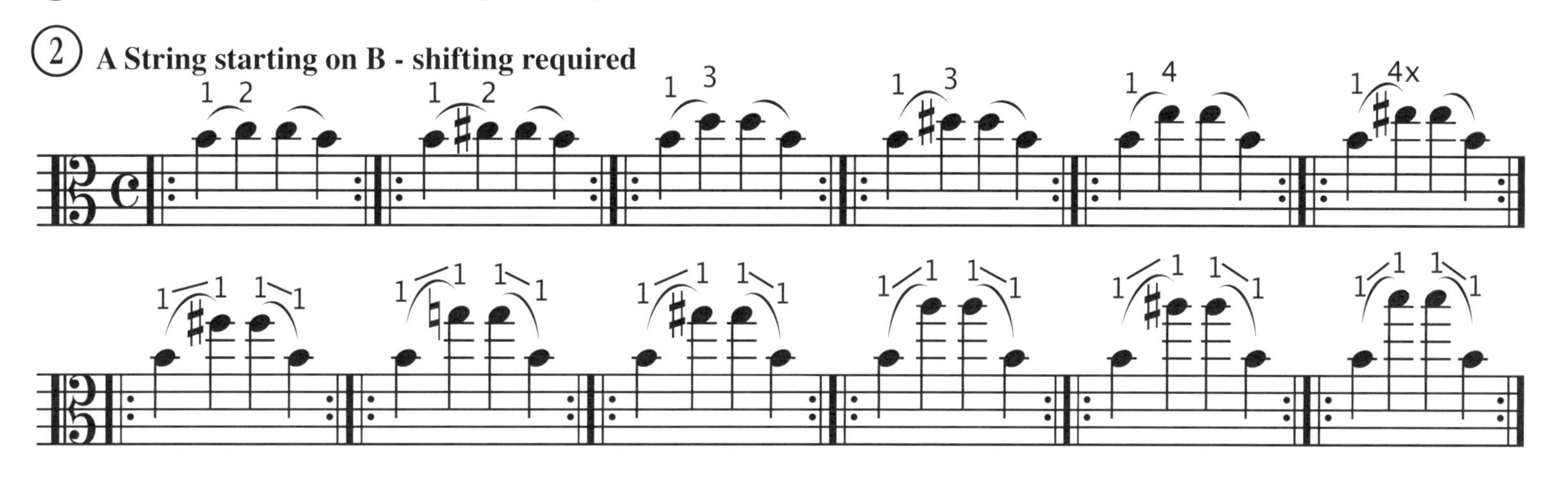

③ **D and A Strings starting on E**

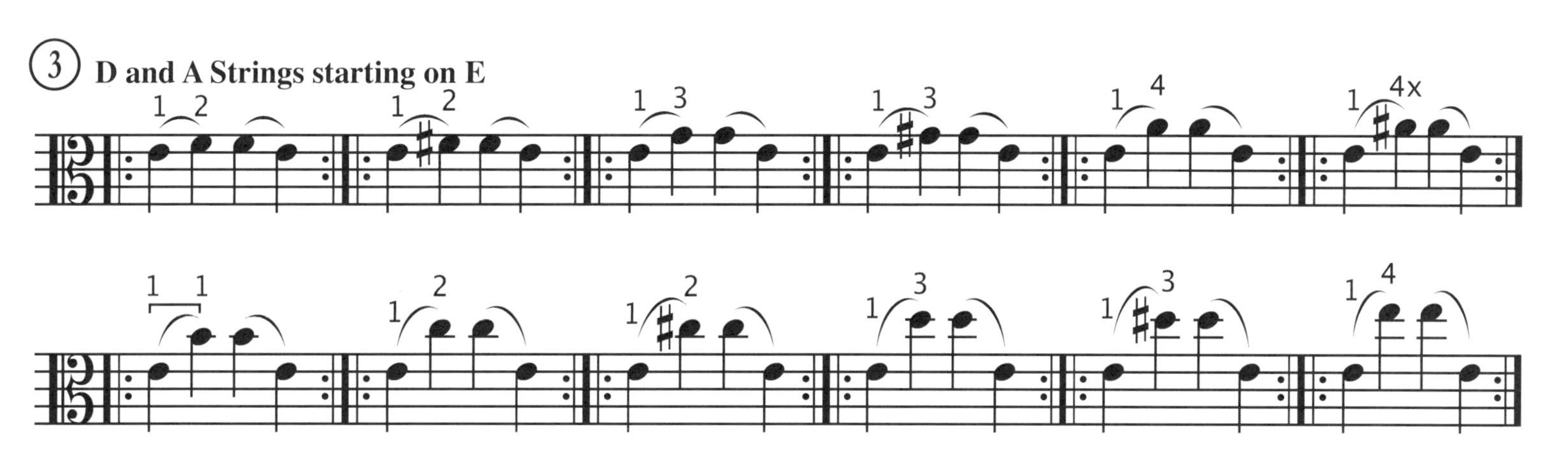

④ **G and D Strings starting on A**

⑤ **C and G Strings starting on D - Violas and Cellos only**

Cello Fingerboard Geography

Shifting Required

♩ = 60

① Violins and Basses on E string, starting on F♯

② A String starting on B

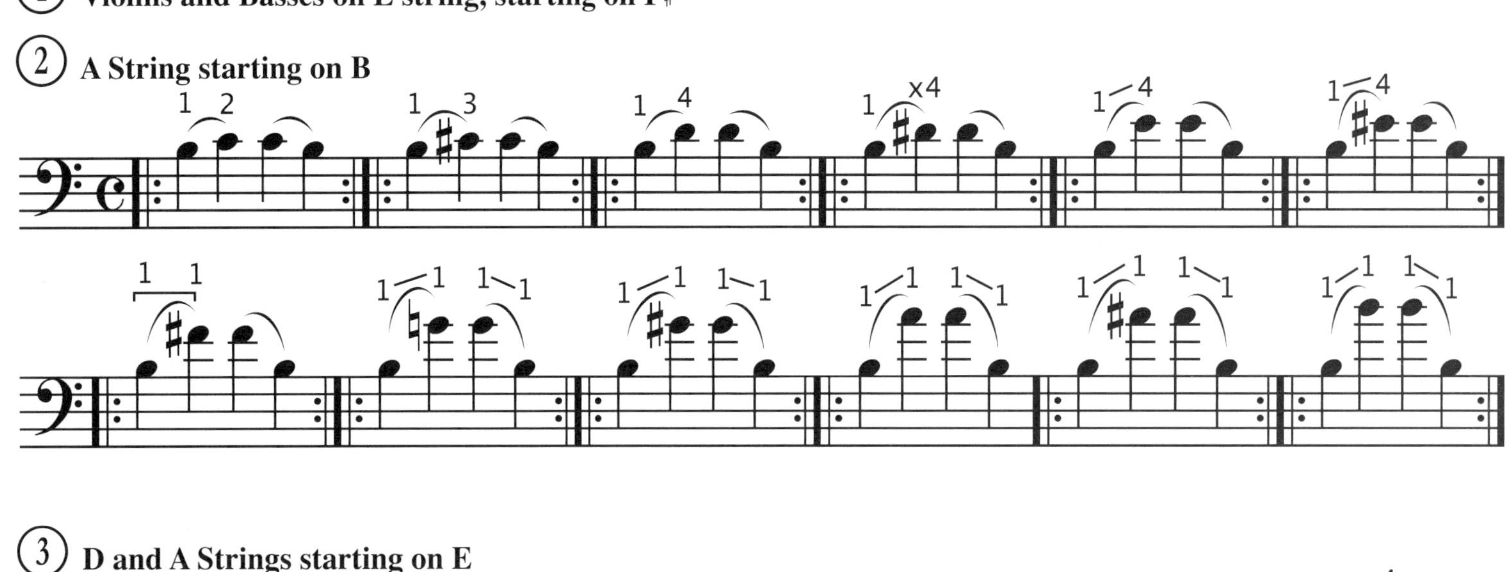

③ D and A Strings starting on E

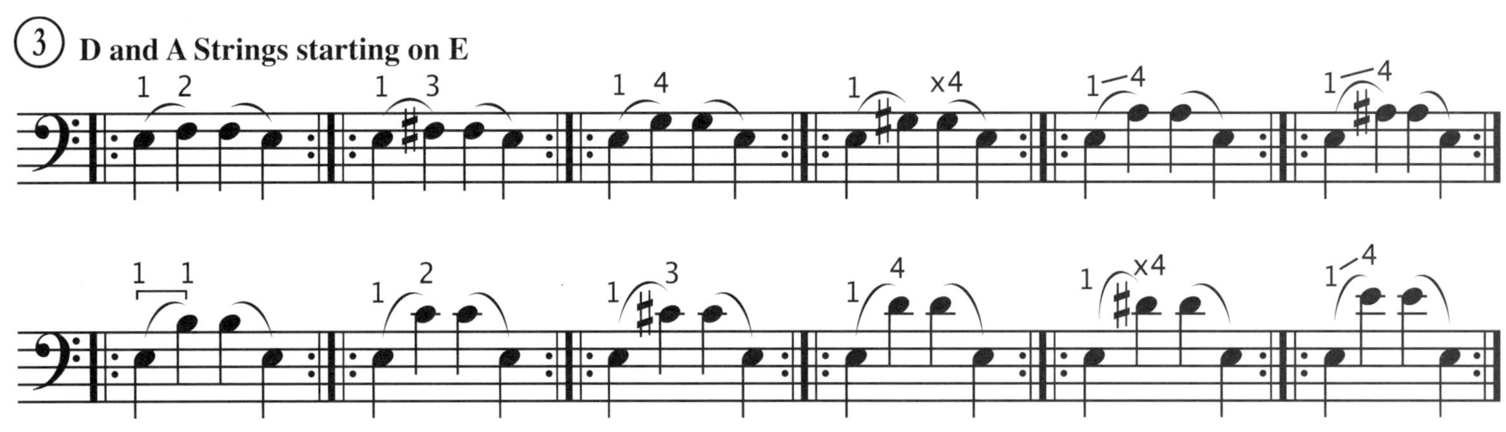

④ G and D Strings, starting on A

⑤ C and G Strings, starting on D - Violas and Cellos only

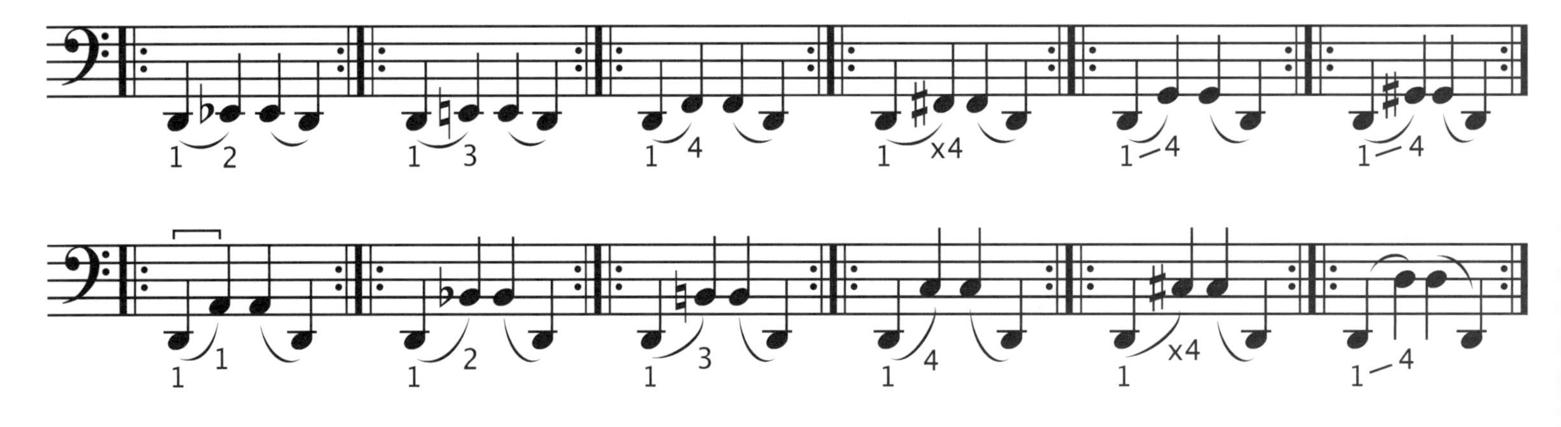

Bass Fingerboard Geography

Shifting Required

♩ = 60

(1) **Basses on E and A Strings starting on F♯; Violins on E String starting on F♯**

(5) **C and G Strings starting on D - Violas and Cellos only**

Part 4: No Fear Shifting with Fingerboard Geography

When introducing shifting, the string player's left hand should be loose and relaxed, gliding easily up and down the fingerboard. Harmonic Exercises one pages 32 and 33 relieve any left hand tension and should be played with full, legato bows. They can be played with all four finger patterns. Next, repeat Fingerboard Geography, an already familiar exercise, with shifts on pages 34 and 35. The first time this shifting system is used, students will shift all the way to 8th position! The violinist's left arm should rotate to the right, bringing the hand up and on top of the instrument for the high positions. Less advanced students can play the exercises in one position, providing a solid tonal foundation, while more advanced ones learn to shift. These exercises can be started on any finger and transposed into any position. Once learned, they are easily played by rote. Some examples:

Shifting 2nd to 9th Position:

Shifting 3rd to 10th Position:

Combining Finger Patterns with Fingerboard Geography

With imagination, teachers and students can combine shifts and patterns in dozens of different ways.

Shift a minor 3rd, then play the Red Finger Pattern:

Shift a Perfect 5th, then play the Yellow Finger Pattern:

Additional Exercises

Shifting to Harmonics on A and D Strings

Play on all 4 strings with all 4 Finger Patterns.

♩ = 60
1 Cello A String in Tenor Clef
2 Cello D String
1 Bass A String
2 Bass D String
Play on all 4 strings with all 4 Finger Patterns.

No Fear Shifting
1st Finger on D String

Play on all 4 strings with all 4 Finger Patterns.

No Fear Shifting
1st Finger on D String

Play on all 4 strings with all 4 Finger Patterns.

Based in Estes Park, Colorado, violinist and violist Barbara Barber is internationally known as a recording artist, pedagogue, publisher, consultant, adjudicator, editor, and author. She has taught and concertized at conferences, institutes and workshops across the United States, and in Canada, Mexico, El Salvador, Brazil, Peru, Australia, New Zealand, Korea, Taiwan, Hong Kong, Japan, Italy, Ireland, Finland, Sweden, and Bermuda. She has appeared as soloist with orchestras in the United States, Mexico, and Brazil. She received her B.M. and M.M. degrees in violin performance at Texas Tech University and has taught violin and violin pedagogy at Texas Tech University, Texas Christian University, and the University of Colorado in Boulder. Active in the American String Teachers Association and the Suzuki Association of the Americas, Barbara Barber has been recognized for her many articles, presentations and roles on advisory and editorial boards. She was chair of the Violin Committee for the revision of the 2003 ASTA *String Syllabus* and is a Registered Violin Teacher Trainer and past board member of the SAA. Her 28 books and CDs—*Solos For Young Violinists, Solos For Young Violists, Scales For Advanced Violinists, Scales for Advanced Violists, Twinkle Variations Festival Arrangement, String Class Fingerboard Geography,* and *Violin Fingerboard Geography*—are published by her company, Preludio Music Inc., and distributed exclusively by Alfred Publishing Company. More than 300,000 of her books and recordings have been sold worldwide. She has also released a CD with Brian Lewis and Michael McLean entitled *Care To Tango?* (Oak Cliff Publishing) and has performed with the Fort Worth Symphony, Dallas Chamber Orchestra, Boulder Philharmonic, Sinfonia of Colorado and Longmont Symphony. Ms. Barber maintains a private studio in Estes Park and Boulder.